Praise for *Your Cat &* (

"I first heard the title poem when Mary read it during a panel discussion, and appreciated its imagination and wry humor. Many of the poems in this book, especially the ones about cats and dinosaurs and other animals, do have a mordant kind of humor, but many more are deadly serious and concerned with larger matters. The book is a huge banquet of food for thought, as well as a display of poetic virtuosity and intense emotional complexity."

Joe Haldeman

"The stunning menagerie Mary Turzillo creates in *Your Cat & Other Space Aliens* not only contains strange cats, but includes rats, mollusks, raccoons, hamsters, crows, a wooly mammoth, a tyrannosaur, and directly or by analogy, that strangest animal of all, human beings. With wit, verve, eccentricity, and brilliance, Turzillo uses her poetry to spin intense tales that portray the dynamics of both personal and familial relationships. At times, *Your Cat & Other Space Aliens* will make you laugh out loud; at times, it may even make you cry. This is a superbly rich collection of speculative poetry."

Bruce Boston, author of *The Guardener's Tale*

Five Reasons Mary Turzillo is a Great Poet
 1) She can be funny.
2) She can be creepy.
3) She can be, on occasion (see, for instance, "God's Savagery in a
        Hospital Corridor"), heart-rending.
4) She combines speculation and striking imagery with a variety of
        forms. Not a one-trick pony.
5) There is an outside chance she is a space alien so it's a good idea
        to say nice things about her.
    -            **Darrell Schweitzer, Poet, Fantasist, Sorcerer**

A marvelous, sometimes humorous, often jolting collection conjured in various forms from Turzillo's multi-faceted perspective. Herein, you'll find poems dappled with lines such as: "He drinks gravity, eats the sky." (Hawk) "She can unwilt flowers on the graves." (Human) "Sirens are thirsty tonight/ In the brine, they lap you like kittens." (Alien) You read these visions feeling very much like you're tripping with a psychic savant, until finally, "The child winds down, his fancy/ flown over rooftops, beyond Mars/ into the dark between the stars." In Turzillo's worlds, you are that child.

Marge Simon, author of *Like Birds in the Rain*

"I love Turzillo's poetry. She makes us see the world at odd angles, gives us a kaleidoscope of domestic and alien grinding up against each other as we turn the pages."

Carolyn Clink, author of *Much Slower Than Light*

Warning: If you think you know all there is to know about your cat (or your husband) then Mary Turzillo's *Your Cat & Other Space Aliens* might just change your mind. Turzillo's gently wry collection of poems blurs the not-so-fine line between humans and not. Her gift is to question our assumptions about cats and other exotic species by limning them with just enough reality to generate a shock of recognition. A wild and crazy mix of everyday life, cats with attitude, cats with dialects, cats with a sex life jumbled in with heaven, hospitals, racoons--anything in the natural world is fair game here— makes this collection a fantasy seekers' delight.

Laura Kennelly, author of A Certain Attitude

Your Cat
&
Other Space Aliens

Mary Turzillo

To Cilla —
Prut,
Mary Turzillo

Professional Reading Series
vanZeno Press
Cleveland, Ohio
Berlin, Connecticut

ISBN: 978-0-9789244-0-9

Geoffrey Landis, Cover Art
Mike Benveniste, Cover Photo
Heidi Della Pesca, Cover Design www.nightship.net

To my pride: Jack, Tiffany, and Geoffrey

Table of Contents

One

Two

Three

Four

Ten

Eleven

Twelve

one

FAQ

Is death contagious?
Death is transmitted by a spirochete endemic to fresh peaches,
phytoplankton, and dreams of empty houses.

Does death wear a disguise?
Death has a splendid set of polished pewter teeth, worn only at the
decease of royal infants.

*Is it true that a new dessert incorporates sugar, creme fraiche, and crystallized
death? What is the calorie count per hundred grams?*
You would find that fatiguing.

*Is it polite to hum along if the bereaved bursts into flames? Should one intervene
before the etheric stage?*
Yes, and never.

*I have seen skeins of gray linen draped on bare trees. Are these sacs of freshly laid
death eggs?*
One should not offend the modesty of mothers.

Might one dance with death at an afternoon tea and still call oneself holy?
If decorously clad.

*What is death's favorite beverage? Should bottles of absinthe be concealed when
death visits?*
Absinthe is entirely correct, garnished with fresh thujone.

Can death estivate in the shells of the fighting conch?
In temperate zones.

Does death preen before mirrors staged in infinite regression?
Wouldn't you?

*If death is seen walking on an interstate carrying a leaking gas can, should one
offer assistance?*
How could you resist?

Is it true that if you draw four deuces in a row, or if you fail to promote an eligible pawn, death will slash your hamstrings?
This is a superstition promoted by Borges cultists and the Penitentes.

Does death experience orgasm?
Only if you like.

Am I going to die?
No.

Is anybody I know going to die?
Only persons you know very remotely. Your touch confers immunity.

Does the thicket conceal death better at dawn or dusk?
Both.

Does death have a favorite number?
Yes.

Does death have a home town? A native language? A weakness for leibfraumilch?
Yes.

Will I know to close my eyes?
Yes.
Yes.
Yes.

More Ways To Tell If Your Cat Is a Space Alien

1. Your cat came from a pet store in Roswell, New Mexico.

2. You find long distance charges on your telephone bill to area codes the operator has never heard of.

3. You come home to find your cat walking on the ceiling, and your cat just looks at you and says, "Yeah, so?"

4. Your cat goes hunting and brings you home a Little Green Mouse.

5. Your cat's eyes glow in the dark. Even when they're closed.

6. When you scratch your cat behind the ears, you notice she has antennae.

7. Your cat volunteers to remove your brain.

8. You <u>agree</u> to have your cat remove your brain.

9. Your cat can program your computer better than you can.

10. Your cat can program your computer better than your ten-year-old kid can.

11. You discover that your cat has a glitzier Web page than you do.

12. You discover your cat has put you up for adoption on the Internet.

13. UPS arrives at your front door with a cage to take you to your new owner -- on 51 Pegasi Prime.

4

Signs You're in Trouble

1. The tide goes out unexpectedly, way, way out, and you can see parts of the sea-bottom you never saw before. You go out to collect shells.

2. The sun rises in the west.

3. Radio broadcasts from the opposite hemisphere have ceased.

4. Your child's imaginary friend suggests that he bring him your microwave, your cell phone, your laptop computer, and a small amount of plutonium.

5. There's nothing on TV except movies about weird talking green cats, and all the channels are showing the same movie.

6. Your parrot learns how to use a satellite phone.

7. The neighbors have silently gathered around your house and they're all holding rocks.

8. Everybody has taken to wearing sunglasses, even while taking a shower or in bed.

9. Noticing a peculiar odor, you go down in your basement and meet a couple of people you were pretty sure were dead.

10. The aliens land in your front yard, and they ignore you while having long conversations with a group of centipedes on your lawn ornament.

11. You awake one morning and notice a three-yard long paw with retractable claws visible from your bedroom window.

12. Frightening creatures with only two legs have landed on your planet. Each carries a tube which shoots beams of bright light. Most frightening, each has only one head.

Dark of the Moon

Whiskers smelling of milk and tuna,
he slinks into his mistress's bedroom
intent on rubbing against her legs
and, since he is tonight her same species,
further up. Beware, werecat's mistress,
the front claws, the barbed penis.

Yanked from the seafood tank,
eyestalks trembling in terror,
to be boiled alive, smothered in butter --
but, saved by the dark of the moon,
the werelobster leaps out of the pot.

She sings her high whine
when the moon goes full,
party crasher who slips through torn screens:
be sure to seal your door
lest your blood flow
to a weremosquito.

help me help me
get revenge says he,
brandishing anti-people spray.
Tonight the dark makes me a man
to swat, to poison you.
At last I avenge my murdered maggots --
I, werefly.

Past Lives

She started out as a dinosaur coprolite.
That life over, but well lived,
she became a now-extinct type of wild carrot.
Then an early mammal, just two inches long,
not very cute, but toothy.

Oops. Bad karma cut her down
until she was a rock in a comet that visited the sun
only once every ten thousand years.
Humans were there the nth time she got back,
but did she get a shot at that? No,
she was a rock in a pasture wall, sandstone.
It wore away, finally, kicked by small boys
into thousands of pebbles, each too small,
for a soul of her caliber.
Life as a blacksnake ennobled her spirit,
so next she was a richly illuminated
Book of Hours, done for the Countess Mervielle.
In that life, she was soul-mate
to a brilliant sword lost to the Saracens.
Alas, they never met,
but knew and loved each other by fame.
The book and the sword lived centuries, deteriorating,
until her soul, dying ennobled and strengthened,
was born into a '65 Cadillac, handsome with fins.
In that life she was male, and her love
(who had been a sword) was a loom
owned by a Navaho weaver with tuberculosis.
They were both junked. And now she sits before me,
a fine computer full of service, to man and to God.
I've lost track of her lover.

Perhaps in some later life she'll live on an Ashram,
human at last, or be the Empress of Cats,
or a program for tracking tornadoes,
or a snail, or a dolphin, or nothing at all.

two

Road Kill

The roadkilled pizza box
will lie scrunched flat by two tire treads.
Late for class, you see pink-gray petal-pointy ears.
You slam on brakes.

You will hit the horn
but the lid of the box will only stir
and when you roll down the window you hear
heartbroken tiny screams
and <u>oh, damn it!</u> you jam the car in park.

The kitten will scream louder now he sees you
and when you move the box, you see
he is bleeding, hind quarters maybe paralyzed.

Avoiding filthy brown and bloody smears
you scoop him onto the box lid
and he will scream at you
help me leave me alone you're killing me help help.

Only later
after his miraculous cure by leftover swordfish,
will it occur to you that he sent out for you,
had you boxed and delivered
and he gets to keep the tip.

Rat

It was midnight but
she called up her friend cause when her ex-husband left he
punched a hole in the drywall and
now a month later a rat used the hole to move in.

So her friend came over and
set humane traps all over the basement and then it was two a.m. so he
started biting her neck and they
went to bed then and woke up at three and
the twins were standing at the
foot of the bed saying
mommy mommy we want to come into your bed cause
we're scared of the rat so they
crawled into bed with her and him. And
the kids left the bedroom door open so
the dog
came in and snuffled and vaulted into the bed but
the kids didn't wake up so
she and he fell back asleep.   And
it was four thirty when
she heard scurrying and he didn't wake up and
the twins didn't wake up and
even the dog didn't wake up and something scuttled up
into the bed and she felt its long tail as
it settled against her and
she knew it was the
rat.

Hamsters

They have cunning beady eyes and soft fur and they
burrow in the upholstery
and create pee messes and they
smell and have to be
fed daily and we
can't be hiring a sitter for the
hamsters when we go away, now can we?
Stop looking at me
that way. It will do no good. You are three,
almost four years old and the
hamster you are holding has tiny
soft feet that pat all over your hand when she
tries to get loose in the sofa so she
can hide in there and breed while we
look for her.
But
the real reason we
are not getting a hamster is that after three
or four months they
roll over and stop moving, they
die
and I am not ready to explain that one to you
so stop looking at me
like that. There Will Be No Hamsters in this house no
mortal things   nothing to educate you
about The End   nothing to die
except Me
and You.

Tiptree

Fourteen days you scrabbled at the bricks
chittering in anger and fear, wanting the mother
who had deserted you in my chimney.

Perhaps she had carried the rest of her litter
like masked kittens in her human mouth
into the neighborhood to survive on my garbage.
Or maybe you climbed the Christmas tree
we bought for my daughter when she was four,
planted and grown huge at the corner of the house.
Then you hopped to the roof, surveyed the neighborhood
and fell two stories to your prison above my grate.

You must have lived on rainwater and bird droppings.
You must have forgotten the sun.
You must have wondered why nobody came for you,
not even me, whose voice you heard,
and who listened every night in growing fear.

I live in the country, alone.
My daughter battles invisible demons
in a city lair, and gestates a monster child.
She would be free of it; I fear for its life,
knowing its father, knowing the mutagens,
knowing I must know and love and foster this baby
when it comes and she abandons it, as she will.

You were a ghost.
You were a rat.
You were the wind.
You were chimney swifts or rabid bats.
You were hallucination.
You were a litter of nightmares.

The chimney sweep came dressed all in crisp ticking
white and blue, with his vacuum and sprays.
He shone his light,
drew diagrams of my chimney's secret chambers, then
declared you had gone long ago,
or that you came by night and left by day.
He censed my fireplace with magic perfumes
and put a screen over the top
so you could not return.

He spoke kindly of little animals,
I wanted to marry him to my daughter.
But before he left, his assistant
slashed his thumb to the bone
and bled like a miscarriage
while I dialed 911, 911.

While they were there, you hid in the soot.
After they left, you waited till dusk, then chittered,
your tiny human hands beating against the flue.
Feed me! Free me! Give me a drink! I'm afraid!

I was alone. I was hallucinating.
but my dog heard you, too, so I knew
I was not mad.

I called the sweep back. Next day he saw
your small bandit face and pointed nose.
He admitted I was not dreaming.
He used firecrackers, Heavy Metal, ammonia fumes
to drive you up the chimney,
out of my life.

Surely, he told me, it is gone now.
I will replace the screen, and there will be peace.

But you were not gone. You were hungrier
and more terrified than ever.
And weaker. You were silent for three days,
lying perhaps in a dirty ball
in a nest of hair left from your mother's belly
or torn from your own breast in your despair.
Then it began again. Chitter chitter chitter
bang bang bang

I knew I must deliver you.
My friends spoke of magics to begone you,
of gluetraps, of 900 numbers, of heroic naturalists,
the kind of advice
they gave me about my daughter, and just as useless.

I put by the hearth a cage, leather gloves,
a thick jacket, boots, a hockey mask.
And when you chittered that next night
I opened the flue and saw
first your small imploring hands,
then your masked face, full of pleading.

We were old friends now; you knew my voice,
smelled my smell, and you were frantic
to be fed, to drink, to be free,
to be mothered.

At that moment, I could have made you a pet
like the raccoon my grandmother had when she was ten.
I could have fed you crackers and apples.
You could have lived with my dog.
I could have found a vet brave enough to tend you.
I could have named you Tiptree
after a dead woman who spun wonders
and took the name of a raccoon.

But I didn't.
I reached up like a brutal obstetrician,
grabbed your small forepaw,
yanked you out, and threw you in the cage.
You were delivered.
I gave you a cookie and took you to Mosquito Lake.

When you finally decided
I would never give you another cookie,
you hopped out into the dusk,
and among the pine needles
you used your hands, that belonged
to a crippled filthy child,
to dig grubs in the interesting dirt.

And I went home and awaited the call from my daughter,
who lives in the city
with her addict and her sorrows.

Unaided, I have exorcised my hearth.
I have delivered you
and I will hear you no more.

LaBrea Tar Pits, Early Summer, Dinnertime

Hungry, curious.
You have cubs to feed.
Those sharp fumes are just tang,
drool-provoking lure for that sloth struggling in black treacle,
still alive, marrow still hot and creamy.
You are no fool. Your pads stuck last winter
to the black ground where the main course screams.
But still you minced in, light as a bird,
and sank fangs into that antelope.
The black gum held you up then.
And again you are hungry,
your cubs hungry,
fangs no longer fitting
either side your shriveling dugs.
Yesterday the smaller cub drew blood
and its eyes said it found the blood good.
So, place your pad, delicate as a bird's beak,
in hot mephitic goo.
It sticks, but dinner calls.
If God was invented before this morning
he is no vegetarian.

Corn Snake

Arcing like live clay,
yellow as pollen,
suave leather against my fingers,
you are not very smart
not smart in my terms
only distantly related to a plesiosaur,
but when you finally found that mouse
with your clever tongue touching the path
then tucking into the twin slits
where you read
ads for meat, small and delicious,
you were sufficient to feel
its heat on your cheeks
its fur against your long long belly
you hugged it though your brain lacks lobes for love
and it released its high mammalian grip on the cosmos
to be meat, a wriggly bone ecstasy for you:
down the hatch.
It may be more evolved, but consider:
in the end, all you or I have
is our need.

Mollusks

Mollusks don't screw
each other up.
They're a calmer phylum altogether.
Clams have less teen pregnancy
and when did an oyster ever go postal?

Think of their defense program:
they only give in when dropped from two hundred feet
or plunged in boiling water.

Dictatorships?
They don't need them --
oligarchy or democracy, either.
I bet
they don't even have weird cults.

I'd love to be a mollusk.
Wouldn't you?
What grand stability.

Their space program
is on hold.

Consolations of Bast

She shivers:
alone in her huge crib,
longing for sleep if she knew what it was.
They
have left her forever.
She wails and the night grinds on,
until the cat comes,
purrs her to sleep.

Heavy
in her arms is
the cat,
perhaps a different cat.
Tears
fall on its indifferent head.
She sobs:
stone-hearted boy!
It purrs.
The hum makes her lose
the thread of her grief.

Her baby screams
with fever;
and so many bills due.
She lies waiting for
dawn and catastrophe.
Please, please,
just let me sleep. So
the cat kneads her chest
and she sinks
into reverie.

The dying
feel warmth,
heavy as a baby, on their chests.
Someone
has left open
the door to the

Home
and the cat,
a different cat surely,
holds down
the old woman's sorrow
its rasp
licking away
only bad memories.

And in the open coffin,
the undertaker's cat
keeps the dead company,
half asleep,
purring:
she does not
go alone.

three

Check Out Madonna

Check out the kid,
maybe five, begs muh muh muh uh buh.
shows Mom the magazines,
candy bars, Hello Kitty with a yellow REDUCED sticker.
English with no T's or D's or L's or --
maybe that membrane under her little tongue--,
tongue-tied, that's it.

Why hasn't the mother -- ?
Check her out. Cliché blond hair pulled back
so tight it's got to hurt.
Body hidden under her sweat suit. Clean. White. Worn.
The wordless girl pulls at her.

Check out what the mother's buying.
Diapers? Jeans? Hello Kitty? No.

Seven different diet aids:
vitamins, diuretics, bulk fillers, and PPA,
which surely killed my appetite
when I took it for sinus.
Also a book: TEN NEW DIETS! ONE WILL WORK FOR YOU!

She's not fat. Thinner than I am.
Good-looking, if her hands didn't shake,
except for that birthmark above her eye.

Look again: not a birthmark. A rug burn, oozing blood.
Who has done these things to you? I want to ask.
But he's probably waiting in the car.
Waiting for her to get skinny, to look like Miss February:
five foot ten ("I <u>love</u> skiing") and a hundred five pounds, yeah, sure.
Honey, Miss February's tits each weigh fifteen pounds.
The kid pulls at her arm.
She pays for the last item in her cart,
a No Fat, Calorie Reduced Health/Slim Bar.

Artificially Sweetened.

Play/Ground

In kindergarten, I got my shoe stuck
in the merry-go-round pump
and bent my foot at a scary angle
so I couldn't teeter-totter all summer
because my cast would get dirty.
The slide was okay except for the mud at the bottom
and the time it zoom-burned my arm.
Janey went over the bars on the swing.
The nuns said she'd fall and break her spine and be put in an iron lung,
but she didn't. She just said, "AAIEEEE!"
and lost her shoe when she jumped off the bottom.
Under the jungle gym
boys screamed "I see Janey's *underpants!*"
but the rat-faced nun was scared of the boys
so Janey was the one made to stand at the brick wall
where they put the bad ones
even in winter when you stood on one leg
to keep the other warm under uniform skirt
and your toes
slowly turned
to ice-cube kisses.

Two Girls Escaped

Two girls, escaped from Sacred Heart,
corner of Elm and Vine:
the brunette's jeans pocket bulges
with Camels stolen from her dad.
Her skateboard owns the street.
The lank-haired redhead
wears a grubby polyester skirt
too short (last year's church dress),
and flaunts her stained panties
when she mounts the bike.

(It's a boy's bike.)

They don't care.
What if you had an accident, girl?
They ride over the curb, screaming,
and the redhead's knee wears a bleeding scab.
In the hospital the doctor
would see your dirty underpants.

They couldn't care less.
They spend their first blood
vaulting picket fences.

God's Savagery in a Hospital Corridor

I witness God's savagery in a corridor
of Rainbow Baby and Children's Hospital
where my boy is under treatment for depression
stemming from his long struggle with diabetes.
A handsome couple stagger down the hall
overcome, not able to contain their hysteria
sobs audible even after they round the corner.
I don't know who will drive them home;
I don't know what killed their child, but I know Who.
I go up the elevator to the Behavior Ward
where my son stays, despondent that medicos have no cure
though they promised one in five, at the most ten years,
and that was twelve years ago. I smooth my face, then open his door.
Cheer up, I say. Things could be worse.
Yes, he says, things could get much worse.

Suppose Heaven

Suppose heaven
is a grocery store big as a town in Texas
where you wander looking for the right kind of apples,

or suppose it's a field of rye
under a hot July sun where you smell the juice of bruised blades
and the wind soughs and subsides, soughs and subsides,
nearly drowned by the susurrus of crickets
filling your ears with their world, banishing whatever you can't see
beyond the ocean of rye horizon to horizon.

Suppose heaven is a hotel lobby
where you are waiting in line behind a woman with a red steamer trunk
while your son waits dressed in a costume for the masquerade
holding a walking stick with a cat's head
and outside night gathers and a storm threatens.

Would you be able to walk out of that grocery,
back to the parking lot in the sun, back to your car, your driveway,
up the steps, carrying a bag of apples and cat food and chicken breasts?
Would there be a world outside the field of rye,
something beyond the green whispering horizon?
Would the woman with the steamer trunk ever get her room,
would your turn at the desk come, you gather your son up,
take him to the room to preen his theatrical gear,
go out to a chinese restaurant, watch the masquerade,
sleep, get up, breakfast, check out?

Would there be a home to go home to in these heavens,
places of bills and argumentative in-laws, Christmas lists and plumbing?
Would you eat the apples, put a Band-aid on the cut you got from the
sharp grass?
Would your son grow up and find the news story of the masquerade,
smoothing the prize ribbon under his hard hands ?

Or would there be forever Now,
looking out the window to the cars moving endlessly in and out of the
parking lot,
to the sun stuck forever a few degrees from overhead
and the moon drifting pale white on blue like a sliver of soap in a blue
tub?
or your son forever watching, waiting for you to check in,
and you wondering what he thinks as he becomes Prince of Tigers?

Suppose heaven is watching forever and ever an endless loop of the past,
cars seen from the hotel window, streaming streaming past
sun glaring from their windows, then rain, then darkness,
lights passing and the hiss of their tires just audible
like the sound of eternity counted in seconds.

How to Pick Berries
Instructions for my son

First you must find a patch
scope it out, maybe remember from last July
Certain berries grow better in July, some in August

They will grow where it is moist but sunny
on the edge of orchards
along sunlit paths.

The best berries may be off the path
hard to reach but more abundant

You must not confuse
blackberries with other types
toxic or just not that sweet:

elderberry, snowberry,
even the burrs on burdock can be mistaken
from a distance. Avoid them.

Then you must gird yourself for the three enemies:
poison ivy, thorns, and mosquitoes.

The ivy has three leaves,
just like the berry bush, but you will soon
distinguish rough berry leaves
from shiny smooth poison ivy.

Then there are thorns. Some advise
wearing long pants, long sleeves, even gloves.
Otherwise they will prick you, like an cat impatient for cream.

Mosquitoes, like sirens, will sing to you.
Swat them and your blood will mark your arm, red as juice.

The best berries are dark and full
warm from the sun. Each berry is different.
Some so ripe they fall into your hand
or into the bramble underfoot.

Others will be red and hard, or withered.
These will be sour.
You can tell only by touching which is the best.

The old style collector
will use a sauce pan, holding it under the branch
but the younger will avoid tragic spills
with a plastic bag.

You will have moments of sweetness
sour moments,
moments when your arm is caught in the thorns
and you disentangle with pain,
moments competing with another picker
or with a sudden snake or catbird.
Ignore them, as rival tomcats or religious fanatics
hissing and scolding you from bliss.

Persevere, son. Bring home a mess
enough for a pie.

Later, your wounds washed and your hands stained purple
You will sit at the table and feast.

four

Foreigner

"There is," they told her, "an Earthman in the city."
In far Al Baldah, in a city on the single world circling pi,
in the ancient books the whole sector called the Azure Dragon.
She, scientist in the field, recording customs,
knew the city, so
she found the Earthman. But natives
whose small planet's brotherhood
had long since blended languages, flattened even dialects,
didn't tell her
the two, Earthwoman and Earthman,
spoke different tongues.
Nonetheless, she found him.
He invited her, by courtly gestures,
to his digs in the burned-out center of the old city.
His furniture alien, brought from worlds
in the Tiger sector, furs, figurines--she ran her fingers,
jewel-tipped in honor
of two Earthlings met so far from Earth,
over alien skins, carpets, bone statues,
chrysoberyl, opaline. He showed her paintings,
artifacts defying Terran genre.
By fat, guttering candles, he fed her tidbits,
which she washed down with Rukbat wine.
She touched books in alien scripts;
he tuned a lute with seven strings and sang.
She asked, "Did you write that?
Were you a minstrel then? Merchant? Mercenary?
Why are you here in the Dragon?
What language do you speak?"
He lay the lute down, took up words again.
In that eulalia uttering courtesy,
he offered her a red silk robe
embroidered with seabeasts not from Earth,
and led her to an inner room.

She left the planet late that month
(the short double lunar month
allowing civil transport only twice a year),
continued charting mating customs of sapient invertebrates
in the Dragon sector--work no doubt engrossing
as hearing Earth songs, alien, far from home;
hearing foreign courtesy;
feeling sculpture feeling
wild pulse on a silk pillow.

Augmented

Fall, 2017

Cat sez
whut tukya so long, I wuz hungry.
I sez
lemme get inna door, will ya? You ain't even dunna dishes.
Cat sez
I don't like ta get wet, the suds don't taste good.
I sez, huh.
ya can't even ansa the phone.
I musta rung ten times. Ya cudda toined the crockpot on.
Goddam cat. Goddam whiny cat.
She stretches, sez
that's the breaks. Ja bring me some livah?
LIVAH!? I sez.
Yuh can't even toin on the goddam crockpot.
LIVAH? I atta put you back on cat chow.
Ain't even paid me back for your
Augmentation Operation.
Huh, she sez. Big deal.
Experiment on innocent felines.
Yeah, I sez. Shudda gotcha spayed instead.
Wyncha getta job? Ya so goddam smart now.
What? asks the cat. Operate a computer keyboard
with these teeny tiny paws?
Yeah, I sez. What, ya think they'd hire you on tv, like Robocat?
Ya too ugly, with that lop ear, I sez.
Cats can't get jobs, she sez. 'Sagainst the child labor laws.
I'm only three years old.
Too bad ya too ugly to peddle ya tail onna street, I sez. It's all ya good for.
More'n you are, she sez.
Sets in ta licking her front paws, in between the toes.
I lose it. Goddam cat.
Here, I sez,
take the rest of this stinkin tunafish and shove it.
And while ya at it, I sez, get out and don't come back.
She looks at me, insolent like.
Wraps her tail around her.

'Sokay, she sez.
I'm booking.
Send me my mail, I'll send a man around in the morning for my stuff.

And I'm looking at an empty door frame.
Jeez.
Round Christmas, I hear she's moved to Soho. Part of a dance act.
Adagio dancing, or maybe it's krumping.
Word is, she's suing me.
Suing
ME--for Wrongful Intelligence.

Early Space Traveler Fantasies

The moon is a saucer of cream;
     what cat will drink it?
The moon is a silver Christmas ornament;
     let me hang it on my tree.
The moon is a porcelain plate;
     I set it with rocket silver.
The moon's a period;
     it ends my sentence.
The moon's a silver nail head;
     my hammer must strike it.
The moon's a pearly bead;
     give me a needle to thread it.
The moon's a zero;
     I am its decimal point.
The moon's the center of a lotus;
     I am drunk on its fragrance.
The moon's the pupil of an eye;
     what does it see? Who does it watch?
The moon's the top of a deep well;
     let me climb to the bright sky.
The moon's a drop of semen on black satin.
     From what lover? What god?

Pasadena, July 4, 1997: Earth Invades Mars

We have come for the firing of 47 pyrotechnic devices.
We have come to watch Sojourner roll down the ramp.
We are part of the invasion of Mars.
You have bought new real estate for our children.
The planets will never be lonely again.

A skateboarder carries a pot of geraniums.
The plumbing, painted to blend with the wall,
resembles a banyan from my dream last night,
trunks an exploding genealogy of science.
A magnificent pregnant woman strides toward me,
past me, her hair black fire.
A man follows, carrying her red huaraches.

Headlines this morning are all about us. Mars -- red Mars!
The children are going to Mars!
At the restaurant, slabs of meat and bright paint
are wrapped in circles clipped out of toweling.
"You should eat the toweling," they advise.
When dessert, cinnamon cherries, comes, our neighbors
(talking about geraniums, or maybe uranium)
set fire to the flowers
and the waiter hastens over to fan the flames.
Fire rises in a column, reddening my plate, my hands.

Your friend (of the very large dish)
picks me up in a hearse painted orange
so full of library books
that he stacks his doctoral dissertation on the roof
realizing three blocks later
that his only draft has blown like big petals all over Colorado Boulevard.

He jumps out, leaving his child to brake the car,
returns with armsful of pink paper --"My valuable documents!" --
and a Picasso knockoff. We drive on.
I carry the Library of Babylon in my lap, my nose crushed into
How To Decipher a Dead Unwritten Tongue
and A Quiet Life Among the Ancient Manticores.

At the house, his wife grumbles,
"The house is a disaster. Excuse it. He's too busy suing people
for stealing his patents."
The outer wall,
has been replaced by a beer mat collection.
He says nothing, meek househusband.

And then tells stories about him and Garcia Lorca, him and Einstein,
how he brewed matté for Borges,
before the old guy went blind.

Later, we look at the stars.
The boy gets peevish,
at our quest for new hunting grounds.
"You want to live in the gravity's prison forever?" I ask, angry
he dare tilt at our fantasies.

He grows quiet, his true father's true son.
Begins to speak of contentment in a cathedral, in a shoe box,
of killing obsolete kittens.
"But we're not killing anything," his father insists.
The mother pours him something bitter and smoky,
says nothing. They love each other, I see.

The child winds down, his fancy
flown over rooftops, beyond Mars,
into the dark between stars.

Hibiscus Island, 2304 AD

When this island shall fall into winter,
datura, hibiscus, oleander will droop,
palms turn gray, live oak drop leaves,
feral cats scurry into any hole
or beg our husbands for a scrap of warm.

When this island shall fall into winter,
manatees will swim into cities
and float exhausted, toward death.
Geckos will shrivel into crevices.
Children will break ice skim on puddles with chapped hands.

When this island shall fall into winter,
sky will turn ashes and pavement,
planting soil cool to permafrost,
salt water crack to dirty glass,
anhingas freeze into the bay.

When this island shall fall into winter,
wolves on two legs will roam,
seek ease for the big pain of gut,
cubs tremble in dark burrows.

We will fell palm trees for their dim heat,
and tribes rise to worship
spider gods who have left their webs,
dead gods in dead power lines.

Boxworld

I am glad I live in Kenning, where the walls are
pliant, membranous, and warm where chance
encounter with a naked elbow or buttock does
not cause the flesh to contract, instead of the
boxes of Derk, so thick, cold, and drafty even
though their manifold walls cramp the interior
space. They say these are modeled on fifties
Plymouths, cubed off by a compactor. They
make them ten yards on a side, but with a tiny
core in which nitroglycerine is exploded, so that
all the layers of reinforced concrete, plaster
lathing, chinese lacquer, gilt and cabbage rose
wallpaper peek through in a random pattern
regarded with pride by the resident, who crawls

in through a door hidden by earthworks. I
spoke to a seamstress from Derk, and she
said she had been to Gameroo, where boxes
are made of laminated straw. In the walls
you can see unripe strawberries,
cornflowers, field phlox, and a few wild
daisies. Gameroo generally smells of
timothy, and the walls of their boxes have
low slits so that they can pass back and forth
backgammon boards, a pastime as dear to
them as dynamiting is to the Derkish. They
cook in dried pumpkins, which seems very
odd to us who use leather bags or petrified
gazelle skulls. And the lady from Derk also
spoke of Claudin, a town which has just
recently become extinct. There they build

canvas, decorated with bird lime and red flashing. Their greatest achievement was a dormitory for monkish scholars, which towered higher and higher until the upper stories loosened, adrift from Earth's gravity, and swam into the stars where they were consumed with nuclear light.

Well, after that, the women of Claudin just seemed to lose heart and the town rapidly lost its will to live. Yes, I'm glad I live in Kenning, where the walls are so warm. Though occasionally a wall -- and this happened once even to one of mine -- gives way with a wet, fragrant pop, admitting access to the neighbor box.

Dash

Your dash clock has four hands and
are those parsecs on the odometer?
And your radio, Jim,
just a little strange. Last night
one station had "The Raven"
read aloud by it author. Last week
you could choose
a play written in porpoise
or telepathic dialogues with Herman Hesse.
On another station,
a live interview with Xantippe and Socrates
on keeping relationships vital,
selections from music of the spheres,
one hand clapping and (performed by
the Martian Tabernacle Quire
and Andromeda Philharmonic)
Fifty Top Hits of the Human Race.

Spin that dial:
news of the week from where
Napoleon, Lee, and Hitler won,
BBC panels on the psychology of sansevieria trifasciata
love sonnets for you, from a woman you never met,
music composed for my funeral,
and, just before signoff,
a compact disc recording of
the Big Bang.

Shouldn't you get that radio fixed?
Or trade the whole damn car in, Jim.
Get a model less in resonance
with elsewhen hums:
dead
absent
neverborn.

five

He was like
a matchbook she carried
around for months in which
someone had written a number
no longer in service.
The phone didn't answer
but the matches still burned.

***

She wasn't afraid
that his beige ways
would finally tire her,
but knowing that white light
makes a rainbow
and brown is what you get
mixing all pigments together,
and thinking maybe that soft sand color
he favored in carpets and clothing
was made of white sun light
washing down earth tones,
the color a million particles
of shells, coral, red, yellow, blue glass, purple snail
make when they make sand,
she was only afraid those colors
might climb back up a sunbeam
burn back into primaries
and
in their bedroom
go suddenly nova.

An Indian woman winds her sari
widdershins, against time,
like a nautilus or a snail shell.
You are pearl pink, bead of sea-water
gathering at the tip
of your helmet shell
not at all like a mollusk
peeking out of its slide-back
stretch silk hole
but taut, smooth
like the tight hard house itself
Let me be the sea and
fish-fragrant, moist breathed,
lap you, toss that shell in
a rising storm.
I will give you seaweed
where you may hide.

***

Foam peanuts float in ditch
like pear blossom petals: white, pure,
incorruptible.

***

Lawnmowers
teach violets

to grow low.

***

December morning

seven a.m.
cold vellum
snow, embossed
with the monogram
of small
red rubber boots
love notes
making promises
only Christmas
might keep.

***

The Deep

In the deeps of forest bottom
leaf fish blink violet eyes
and instant tiny bugs like shrimp larvae
feed trillium stars.

***

Moon, oh luminous companion
who walks beside me and waits politely
if I stop,
listen
to the conversation of these crickets at twilight,
but let us draw our own conclusion.

six

Switchback above Cat's Tail Creek

Her hair was wet, sir, when I pulled her out,
though back at the Moonlight Inn, she used that blow-dry thing.
No, the desk clerk didn't ask to see our license.
He saw plenty kids like us, who knew
in Virginia you only have to be 16
if the bride is expecting.

Emily, her name is. No name for the baby yet.
Now her last name's same as mine, even though --

Emily said, "You're drunk." I wasn't, sir, but I let her drive.

Only she didn't know these sharp switchbacks.

Only four foot of water in Cat's Tail Creek, but she was stunned
and I couldn't get her out quick enough.

I kissed breath into her harder than I did
back on that saggy bed in the Moonlight Inn.
Her chest moved up and down, but when I quit,
it didn't move again.

Then the sirens came, and you, sir. You say
you're cousins with the Mayor,
the old guy that married us?

She isn't even hurt, to look at her. Her neck is so smooth.
And on her cheek, her pretty black hair drying.

seven

If You Loved Me

if you loved me
you would buy me a kiloton of semisweet chocolate
compressed to neutron degeneracy
if you loved me
you'd do genetic engineering
on my former boyfriend and his wife
transforming them into naked mole rats
if you loved me
you would go skinny-dipping in heavy water
letting me ride your shoulders
so I wouldn't get wet
but you don't love me
because if you loved me you'd
rearrange the asteroid belt in the shape of a heart
with my initials on the buckle
you'd win the Nobel prize and give it to me
for my book on cat telekinesis and not mind when people said
you were an idiot for love
but it's real obvious you don't love me
or you'd build a time machine
and we would travel to the beginning of time
so you could bang me
at the moment of the big bang
and not get mad when I said
no no sweetie it's that time of the month
if you really loved me
you'd rocket to Venus and jump off the love-planet
and plummet to your death in my back yard
if you loved me
you'd die you'd just die

Carpe Diem

Marvell knew it:
love before falling asleep
(beneath English roses or under Ohio clay).
In the end, the dying sun
will go nova and burn us
to less than atoms:

so give it to me, lover,
your and my
piece of forever.

Honey, you
popped my cork. You
broke the sound barrier. You
took Little Round Top. You
ungordianed my knot. You
took us ballistic. You
wrote a new ending. We
achieved escape velocity. Now

let's just float.

***

We made poetry
(for Geoff)

All afternoon we made poetry.
Metaphors sparked between our thighs;
you stood me against a wall and allegorized me;
hyperbole ran down our legs and pooled in our socks.
The air was sticky with imagery
and when the phone rang, we knocked it off the hook
because we were in the middle of a sestina.
It was your agent, calling to say he had sold your penis.
We didn't care.
Your penis would fetch more in free verse anyway.

Later, we showered together, scrubbed off the clichés
stuck to us from accidentally brushing a book of porn
(you called it erotica) kept in the bedside vagina.
I caressed your vocabulary with nostalgia and lust,
and we rinsed off the lingering rhyme scheme
amazed how Lady Calliope hunted us down,
ravished us, and ordained us her bawds.

Epithalamion

You pull me out of the darkness, Sun of Morning,
and I warm to your regard. It is a long journey
out of cold which bunches me into a fist.

You are only the brightest star of many for a long time,
then you are the star of my centering.

I grow hair; my volatiles warm; you draw me
and I yearn toward you like an eager virgin,
flying, flying.

A glint on one of your retinue gives me his name:
Hyakutake.
I do not know this. I do not regard
small devices of carbon.

My hair grows; I am your queen,
my love for you is measured in miles per second.
It's been a long time, love.

Shall we dance? Shall it be a wedding dance?
I race down the aisle past your attendants,
flaunting my beauty. My veil is diaphanous, flowing,
glowing, nuptial raiment fit for a cosmic wife.

Now I am hot! Now I am alight!
I fling myself around you,
driven, pulled on gravity's ribbon
heart-racing close to the furnace of your huge love.

Then away.
Must I leave? My momentum says:
> Go, girl, back to the cloud, back to the old neighborhood,
> lurk shyly for ten thousand years, until another time.
> The master will call you again.
> No other star will draw you, ignite you, pull you away.

Love will not be denied;
I am Sun's bride.

eight

Tony

Hawk drops in
swoops down up
power pendulum
in bullet ballet.

He dances on distance
partners his board
spins her under his heels
his leading lady, catwoman, his bitch,
his bride on wheels.

The pipe's his spaceship
stages his zero-G pas de deux
thunders him down, he bottoms
gets back delta V
gives back the sky.

Then up
540, 720,
grinds music
touches coping
rise like exploding
fallen angel rockets
out of the bottom
spinning, dancing
taking air, air, air.

He drinks gravity
eats the sky.

St. E's Emergency

Why do you seem to think
poetry is like vomiting,
and people so greedy for reality as you know it
they peer into the kidney basin
looking for the tenor like a rhinestone stud
you swallowed as a parlor trick,
then having to be taken to St. E's Emergency,
sure it would perforate your tender gut
and work its way through to the heart?
I hope the people at the party liked the trick,
though they may have been a little revolted.
As an orderly on night shift at St. E's,
I really can't get too interested in that stud.
It isn't mine,
any more than your reality is mine,
so take it home and stick it,
along with your other agonies and poses,
in the shoebox you use to keep
subway tokens, cat hair-balls,
expired rabies tags, poison pen letters,
stray buttons, needles, and cracked
marbles.

The telescope

It is enough
to show a child a wild eagle
enough to take children out on a cold dark hill
and show them Halley's gossamer tail,
streaming forever across the sky
long as a woman's life.
It is more than enough.

In the dark dome,
a girl climbs to the eye piece
puts her face to the sky,
and he says, Do you see?
Do you see the Cassini division?
Titan? How many moons
can you see?
How many rings?
And for a long time she looks
then she breathes,
Oh! It really is there,
it really has rings.

And he says,
that's
what I want to hear.

For him, it is enough.

Botanist

Better than the sheb huala that kept their distance
she loved the feral flowers,
long corambes of ivory, cold silk on warm fingers,
pink anthers inside hooded petals, chiming music
even humans could hear,
sepals tender as cheeks, pursed around seedpods
that burst like fireworks when dawn ripens.

When she walked out in the feral garden
their scent made her drunk. Later
she knew she must draw them, search their anatomy.
She took folding chair, penpad and fingerstick,
into the meadow at noon. At sunset,
we found her, dazed by their voices.

Three days of Earth air brought her back.
"Let me paint them," she begged,
Her husband followed her into the garden,
carrying her easel. "Don't touch," she said,
but their eyes were seared shut when they wandered home.

She cut five singing branches, carried them
into her kitchen to paint. The feral flowers drank her mind,
maddened the whole house, and in final defiance
shriveled into dead lavender fists.
"Exquisite," critics judge the two paintings she managed.

No one goes to the feral garden now.
Her paintings are famous. She lies
under blossoms. Their pollen seeks, still seeks,
sight and mind in a human skull.

Some Joys Never Die

Late in my father's life, his appetite
began to fail; decaf coffee, sugar substitute,
and low-fat milk began to pall
beside the joy of suit and countersuit.

Travel was out; late hours made him bilious.
Never a heavy drinker, he said adieu
to whisky, beer, and all his drinking buddies.
Instead of buying rounds, he'd rather sue.

Pleasure of satin sheets and silken thighs
lost their allure; that's just the very flaw
of honored age. And so my father turned
from fleshly pleasures to pleasures of the law.

For in his dotage, wrongs swelled for redress,
and Dad would, worldly cravings finally mastered,
with joy in justice, joy in sweet revenge,
lifting an empty glass, say, "Sue the bastard!"

Theatre Moonie

Brother, who brought you in?
We love you
as you peddle tickets and lies
(cause art is GOOD lies).
Hang lights paint flats have a Dutchman bath
until five am,
sleep on a concrete slab
in the props loft,
live on heath bars coke
bad coffee speed and fritos.
If you're good you're allowed a shower
(cold with no soap cause costume lady
use it to suds some tights).
Mom threw you out of the house:
leave WAY behind family girl friends high school jock friends
wife/husband kids if you had any.
Know your lines? After we open
unlike a real moonie, you get to be normal.
Till then
go in a trance
Jesus won't love you
but Dionysus'll dance in your pants.

Off to the Big Time

she was a star

she let us know

going places FAST

she left years ago

skipped the Milk Train

bound to shine among those

bright lights

she was hot she was spinning

for a travel dress

she wore her

red shift

nine

The Night They Blew the Thinker Up

The night they blew the Thinker up
I was young, hot as a cat.
AIDS hadn't been invented.
Pot was a capital offense
and entirely socially acceptable.
We wore beads and skin. The word love
was caviar in our mouths,
a new taste,
the whole world in a candy wrapper.

The night they blew the Thinker up,
what they were thinking?
Did the police try very hard to find them,
or did they figure
everything was changing and they'd better
kill us all before we got loose
and gnawed the bones of the world right down to chaos?

The night they blew the Thinker up,
we all had alibis.
Couldn't be one of us.
Could it?
Where was Randy? Where was Umlaut?
Old Peppermint Twist? How about Dharma?
Case Tech labs were open all night, and some of us
had strange ideas of the righteous.

The night they blew the Thinker up,
I was sure someday we'd find out who did it,
who massacred Rodin in one boom
just before the evening news.
Or maybe the Thinker blew himself up, like the monk
who made me run to the dictionary
for the word *immolate*, who believed
he could end the pain by his own horrific exit.

I wish I could say I was different after that night,
that I realized how complicated things were
but the fact is, I admire that kid that was me.
I've come down. We changed the world
just a bit, arm-wrestling
Richard Nixon and Lyndon Johnson and the Viet Cong.
But then (and I was wrong)
I thought we could save everything,
the night they blew the Thinker up.

Boxes of Poetry

Boxes marked Sunburst, Niagara Bleach, Fruit Varieties, Trout Apples
slice open with a kitchen knife.
Things inside make me cry.
Inside are my people, my chronic condition.
Buckdancer's Choice, not a first edition.
Holding your Eight Hands,
Coney Island of the Mind, signed eighteen years after I bought it.
J. V. Cunningham's nasty shorts.
Chuck Buck, Diane Wakoski, Kenneth Koch doing a dance on Williams.
A 1948 magazine with a Kenneth Patchen in it.
Wanda Coleman, Toi Derracotte.
A college zine with a perfect Zelazny poem from his Case Western days.
Silverstein, even McKuen. *A Spaniard in the Works.*
More private stuff: only chapbooks by guys I know, guys I knew,
by nurses, cops, angels.

by Tim who killed himself maybe because
my mentor thought his work pretentious.
Coteries I lived in, enmeshed, a secret web.
A college brochure that I almost throw away;
then I see
a photo of me and that angel voice nobody knows, Pap Holmes.
I lived in busy times.

I tell myself, girl, launch your paper boats while the wind is up.
The crooked river runs dark, runs like perfume.
You'll never catch it.

Flowers over Steel

I'll remember the rust belt town that flared and went out in the eighties
as covered with the black soot of steel,
and the leftover boys
who can't do nothing but smoke dope, drink,
and pound their wives to fat scolds or fanatics,
places like Sonny's, where somebody everybody knows got shot
in a fight over a woman neither man cared much about
but where you can still get rotisserie chicken, Texas taters, and Wild
Turkey,
but not skim milk,
and you can send your six-year-old to buy Camels,
city rentals with wells next to their septic tanks,
where the landlord yells at you if you park in the street
and evicts you if you don't,
where the windows upstairs are curtained with paper bags
since they got shot out last Fourth of July,
where you aren't allowed to bring your friend Mike
because he's black and the landlord don't like it, see.

The sidewalks are broken,
covered with broken beer bottles and spit,
blocked with cars with flat tires,
parked there maybe by dead people.

But the thing that surprises me, as I drive my U-Haul away,
to lonely R&B guitar from an upstairs window,
is that in May the flowers will stick up their bright tongues and fingers,
daffodils, tulips, hydrangeas, azaleas, lilacs
and, August nights, fragrant as whorish heaven,
the jimson weed's
defiant trumpet.

Old Poet Calls me Up

Old poet calls me up
says he's lost his poems
his hard drive crashed, do I have copies?

His ex wives might have copies, but he thinks
one of them has a restraining order on him
and the other a bench warrant.

He's drinking a bottle of peppermint flavored beer
he found in the Stop-N-Rob near his house.
Can't stand it, but too broke to throw it away.
I can smell it over the phone.

I might have his poems, maybe in a Jim Beam crate
with my old taxes and my son's crayon drawings of monsters.

There's this one poem, he says, about a dog so wild
his first wife locked him out of the house
until he build a fence to keep it in, which took until four in the AM,
whereupon the dog jumped the fence, then jumped back in,
just to demonstrate he could do it.

And after the dog peed their clean laundry
his son had to stop him from shooting the dog in the city limits
so they took the dog out in the cemetery,
thought he could run it over to save a bullet
but the dog was faster than the car.

And he says, you know there's this one poem
about how the mob was going to break my dad's knees
because I stole the prizes out of the candy machine.

His father sang the Internationale
going through Shaker Heights. Took him to a Wobblie meeting
when he was only five. The police broke it up
after the riot started, and his dad dragged him into the ladies'
and hoisted him through the window to escape.

There's this poem --

And he's singing the Internationale. "Arise, ye prisoners -- "
He was five then, before I was born.

His hard drive crashed.   His songs are gone.
What's he need with a computer? For him
a bottle of bad beer and a telephone
make a time machine.

Metamorphosis of the English Teacher

Today I dress up
to give my Powerful Magic Lecture
on the slow rhythm of the seasons
and the psychedelic effects of lyric poetry.
This requires
a long white robe
and bare feet,
my ridiculous middle-aged brow jammed under a wreath
of myrtle from the dean's tree lawn.

The class stares:,
sleek eyebrows and magenta lids
under red hair, polite and abashed.
Fashionplate Farah, Shy Sheila, Bob Biblehugger
to whom Jesus has told
several things He never mentioned to me.

I prefer Dionysus
who by the way seems to have deserted me today.
I rave, but lack conviction.
My robe slips off my shoulder
and I pull it back,
just like a gesture I once made fun
of old Professor Singer for.
Hey! You think these kids will
ever be good for anything?

Still, I intone:
"Poetry verbalizes
the sublime in human nature.
Our first image of God
was female."

One timid paw:
Will this be on the test?

The Tooth

Pain, pain that has grown with me for thirty years
split by my grinding jaw in the hard nights
by the holding back of harsh words and curses

grows to a sharp angle, aching above my lip,
under my eye, until the pain ripens and I say
now,
now I will give up now I will give my dear tooth
to the smiling surgeon.

He cranks my jaw, he needles my gum,
he pats my arm and tells me it's fine
fine to lose part of myself that I grew, that grew with me.

A clatter on the stainless tray.

It lies like an ivory hand streaked with my blood
washed away, washed away perfect and creamy
and I tell it farewell like my temper
like the clenching, like the angers of past years,
like my life all in a glove of blood.

I am implanted with metal,
like a clockwork bird

until there is nothing left of the child who grew me.
So I move by spaces into the future,
into the dusk of the grave.

She Who Was the Beautiful Helmet Maker's Wife
(after Rodin)

She who shot at hunters on our back acreage,
she who could lift a five-year old girl by her arm,
and drag her screaming into the station wagon,
she who could perform Malaguena and hit high C,
who sang solo Gounod's Ave and could scream curses to terrify
hardhearted children,
she who fought drunk with my father
and chased him around the cooking island with a stainless steel knife,
she who cheered for Rosa Parks
but stopped eating at Rosie's to avoid the gay waiter,
she who populated my childhood nightmares,
she who murdered my kitten:

she lives now in the dark fuzz of blindness and muffled voices,
unable to understand computers or how to use a cell phone,
or to find the History channel on her own TV.

She who my father's friends eyed as tomcats do a cat in heat,
she who dallied with the carpenter thinking we'd never find out,
she who, in her eighties, fought for a 22 pistol with her senile lover Red,

now eats like a dog, food slopping from mouth to dish,
belly bigger than in pregnancy,
jowls slack, skin splotched black and brown.

She who edited our history to make her the heroine,
has forgotten even the lies that exonerate her.

She never killed the kitten or my rabbit.
She never sent my incriminating letters to my best friend's mother.
She never destroyed my sister's dignity.
She never blackmailed our father into disinheriting us.

She who kept diaries of every ensemble she wore
now wears a greasy once-pink robe until her nurse dresses her.

She who pinched grocery money to buy Lilly Pulitzer frocks
now sits in a rocking chair naked but for a towel.

She who was the terrible goddess of our childhood
now is the pitiful dog at our doorstep
beaten by time
                                and we begin to know
both pity, and a different terror.

ten

Mantis

Outside Office-Max, heel- or wheel-ruptured
the mantis lies
crushed, green guts erupted.
They're protected, you know.

I genuflect, curious
 (is he --?)
He is rare,
beauty terrible, smaller
than my hand. He is dead.

I make his bier
an index card. The wives eat their husbands,
the nymphs their sisters,
they disperse by wind. So they are solitary.

Imported by accident, soon seen
as a beneficial predator to eat
Japanese beetles, but so cannibalistic
they are never numerous.

Protected, you know.

Mantis means prophet. You are a Mandarin
among mandrakes. You mantle above your prey,
strike, then mangle, a man-eater.
Your mandible is fearsome, your household manes
are manic gods of a maniac house.
Revered from Mantua to Manila,
your mane a mantilla over your mansard-shaped head.
Quick as a Manx, when your manifold eyes see
miniature prey, you are like a manticore.
Yet, contemplating your intrinsic mana
in repose, you might be intoning a mantra.

Their front claws slash out so quick
they catch a fly before it can buzz.
(Nymph, in thy orisons.)

Yet this one has stained the sidewalk with its ichor.
Monster. Predator. Tigress of insects.

I lay it on its bier on my front porch
that its mana may instruct my house manes
how the mighty
are fallen.
Gnats sing tiny hymns over it
no longer hors d'ouevres for my killer green prophet.

Oneiromantic. Chiromantic. Necromantic.

They're protected, you know.

I leave you in the sun
to your fate.

Gacy

In Jack's dream
we live with John Wayne Gacy.
Something is wrong, Jack says, but I don't seem to care.

Gacy lives on the first floor,
brings home construction workers
who scream, briefly, in false dawn.

Jack says, Mother, we should run,
but it seems okay to me.
The killer can't be interested in us.

Women of a certain age aren't his thing,
and he only uses trick handcuffs.

Trick is, you need the key.

The dog snuffles in the basement dirt
and Jack says he smells something dead in the bathroom.
But I keep saying, oh son, it's okay.

It's hard to get a good rental in this town,
especially when you have cats,
though the cats keep disappearing,

and Jack must be kidding when he says
he feels hot breath
in the night
on the back of his neck.

My Dentist's Son

My dentist's son
whose eyes are blue jewelry
and intricate as a diamond drill,
watches the excavation in my mouth,
with goofy horror.

He is delighted.
A virtuoso actor, he gags
at the stumped tooth
while Dad attempts to crown it.

Such curiosity could burn to the earth's core
or make the universe heave up its entrails.

Hydrangea

I brush my lips in moist
pink white green
suede globe,
my hydrangea
maudlin as a Victorian bedroom.

hydra (blown up with water) ngeas
wilt if you aren't good to them
they need it once a day or more.
It's so dependent, my hydrangea.
If I don't love it with a cup
of water
it goes all limp
the petals lie down
dying!
I rush in: you poor thing
let me love you, here here's WATER WATER
and in minutes it stands up
braver than other flowers
an enormous perky pink head

proud thirsty

Gypsy and the Snake

My husband dreams he goes to a gypsy,
thinks, I'll keep my money unless she's really psychic.

She wants his wedding ring.

What the hell, he has two rings,
gives her one, wedding, not engagement,
squeezed, it changes to a snake.

By its coils, she divines,
as soothsayers with entrails.
S-curve means surprise in the mail; tight loop, old enemies.
But the snake gets away.

Husband and gypsy chase the snake,
under bed, into rainbows cast by crystal,
everywhere snake can slither. They catch it.

But it dies.

The snake dies?
I look at him. Why,
I ask, does the snake die? He shrugs
reminds me, there were two rings.

Sirens

Sirens are thirsty tonight.
In the brine, they lap you like kittens,
coyly pretending to be pretty and helpful.
They suck your tears, your spit,
the plasma from your blood.
They reach out tendrils of singing.
You know you need them --
how can you say no?

They work so hard for you,
dragging with the current,
to pull you under,
to kiss you to breathless,
to take your pleasure,
to slap you against the sand.
You can lie there. It's easy.
You will give what they want.
You will bloat in the tide.

eleven

The Monster's Mother

It shouldn't surprise you
how, born out of her mother Mary's death,
growing up in that household with Doctor Polidori,
running away with her silly genius Shelley,
(for which his wife drowned herself in the Serpentine),
she would have written a tortured romance
about a misshapen thing born from a man,
all those murdered children,
the anguish of a monster without a mate,
because, after all, maybe she could see
down the aisle of years
to the babies that died in her arms
while she tried to milk life back into them,
her husband killed by cold water,
and little Percy, the baby who lived,
so hard for her to keep
when his wicked grandparents
tried to rip him out of her life.

It shouldn't surprise us at all
given the scars on her heart
that in her teenage thriller,
the one she pitied the most
was the monster.

Snow after False Spring, Again

Richard's complaint, another ice age, lasting weeks,
another false hope, false spring.

A skeletal tree fruits with sarcastic crows
discussing the current weather, current assassination.

The tree's a cathedral, the crows dour archbishops:
will no one rid me? Because Richard's too slick.

Groundhogs bed down in clay whether they shadow
or sun. No prognostics, except: Anne will marry again.

Richard will flaunt his hunchback and she will get wet
Will those women never learn?

If winter's discontent, spring is no less than lust
gone mad with hope.

Winter's his element, birds, ravens and crows
his varied nemeses. So when they come back,

Richard's in his closet, stroking his ermine, adding armor,
wondering if batting would double this crown as helmet,

looking through misted glass, cursing the sleet,
wishing a season could last more than a life.

Poor Richard. Until all the blood in England
flows into the Thames, he'll never get warm.

Edward Curtis's Two Zuni Girls at the River, with Pots

No Grecian urns,
no frozen maidenhood,
only the moment, wrapped in dark robes,
ceremonial and cold,
carrying water in the freezing dawn,
one girl's urn depicting antelope and roadrunner:
swiftness frozen as is her grace,
her shivering duty, bringing water.

The other, sister, friend,
balances a pot with zags of lightening,
abstract, aesthetically beyond Keats's urn.

Those girls are dust, never kid yourself.
The pots were thrown from brittle clay,
their impact more ephemeral.
I remember their silent grace
before bending to water,
and so little else of the photo except
they were beautiful.
And someday nobody will look
at the pots or Curtis's image
just as nobody can see those mortal women now.

Curtis tried to freeze beauty,
tried to make the water untasted,
the pots unshattered,
the women unaged,
the morning always bitter and fresh.
He tried to make a Grecian urn,
a Grecian sacrifice
of hooved animals and womanhood.

Edward Curtis's urn is broken, too,
his eye stopped with darkness,
the lid of his coffin shutting off his light.
His vision lives longer,
but not forever.

The pots, fragments now, in museum drawers,
are no unravished brides.
Chemicals fade into paper dust, aesthetics shift.
The image and the pots
tumble down
the river of our memories.
We reach in to seize shards
then tumble into the stream.

Thirteen Ways of Looking at a Blackbird Looking at a Black Cat

I
In the back yard
the only thing moving is a blackbird, me,
and a black cat's eye.

II.
I am of two minds.
The cat has just one idea.

III. The black cat whirled.
Good. Chasing its tail,
it will not chase me.

IV. A black cat and death are one.
A black cat and a bird and death
are one.

V. Which to dread more?
The patty-pat of a cat's paws or
the silence of a cat I don't hear?

VI. The nest was heavy with eggs.
The nest was shadowed with the gaze of
a black cat.

VII. Oh plump women of Pasadena,
do you not see the stalking of birds
in the slinking of cats against your ankles?

VIII. I know the beauty of a blackbird's song,
but I know the dread of a black cat is involved
in what I know.

IX. When the black cat slunk out of sight
it marked the beginning of bad news.

X. At the yowl of black cats courting,
even the bawds of Sunset Strip
would blush deeply.

XI. I flew over the cornfield and fear pierced me
that I mistook the shadow of my wings
for black kittens.

XII. The can opener hums.
The black cat must be begging.

XIII. It was afternoon all afternoon.
It was drizzling and it was going to drizzle.
The cat keeps dry.
This bird stays safe.

Surrogate

I nudge you erect, wool rough against my trunk,
long hair like the mane of humans that ride me.
You have no true father, for when I hankered for a bull
only the man came to me, with his small fist and jarred juices.

Through two turns of seasons, he sang to me,
Precious, you carry life from the ice,
your baby a prize beyond all esteem.
Why should he tell me the worth of my calf?

You are worth more than the world. Beside you
the man is just mud, despite his crooning,
despite sweet fruit he hands my hungry trunk.
I have had calves before, each beyond price.

You look at me, eyes too sharp, legs ready to run.
A baby should be soft, should lean on a mother's legs.
You are strange, beyond the shag of your pelt.
I begin to fear your alien, strong body.

You hunger after I nurse you, after you drain me
with your strong short tongue. So the man feeds you
slops from a hose, milk from stupid cattle,
milk men's children drink. Not my milk.

Yet, small one, you are sturdy,
rooting the ground, looking for grasses
that do not grow here in the camp.
Hungry. Too strong. Why does your hide grow fur?

You will be a rugged cow. The man will take you to Chiang Mai
or a farm further north, wanting to breed you
with something from the ice, as he has done me.
At night I think, if I only had tusks, I might kill you.

But your ancient young eyes tell me, *Mother,*
You saved me from spear-men and ice. My womb
birthed you to a shaggy bull, long dead.
I nudge you forward, love you into the future.

Dinosaurs May Be Ancestors of More than Birds

Paleontologist Dr. Felix Stalker
today unveiled three specimens
thought to prey
on ancestors of birds.
"Logic says," according to Stalker,
"where there's birds,
there's got to be cats."

First specimen:
Acatasaurus. Originally thought vegetarian,
this long-necked ancestor of the Siamese
probably fed on early fish.
Early aquariums may be discovered
 on future digs.

Second:
Velocimouser. This quick-witted
swift catosaur captured prey
by silent stalking, then pouncing.
Clever and voracious, it
may have gone extinct caught off guard
taking naps
after dismembering small mammals.

Most controversial specimen:
Purranosaurus Rex. Note long, rapacious teeth.
Also called Thunder Catosaur because of low rumbling sound
emitted after devouring prey
or shredding furniture.
Small front limbs may not have been
as useless as they look.

Dr. Stalker showed bone fragments
of other catosaurs
"too early to categorize,"
he said. "But tentatively named
Triwhiskerops (note pointed structures
either side its head),

Meowasaurus, good mother catosaur,
Prrtadactyl, Kittycoatlus, and Architsbackterix,
evolutionary blind alleys
nature abandoned when catosaurs
found they could not leap
forty feet. And finally the ancestor of the domestic feline:
Ankylorubbosaur.
Dr. Stalker plans next summer
to seek fossils
of a species
believed to prey on catosaurs:
the Fidonychus.

The Tyrannosaur under 81st and 7th Avenue

Spelunkers from elsewhere
will explore earth's caves
and find, embedded in tiles,
beauty blurred by eons,
the Tyrannosaur at 81st and 7th Ave

and castings of Dunkleosteus,
Pterodactyl, Smilodon, and Hadrosaur
made to give young bipeds a taste of
dead, real monsters above.

Symbols: NEW YORK MUSEUM OF NATURAL HISTORY
on the lintel of the once great hall of bones above,
would inform them, except
glaciers scoured Manhattan bald.
They will suppose these dead artists
lived always underground.

Subway T-Rex will shake their beliefs,
those who had thought that Biped Cavers lived
millions of years after Thunder Lizard

As at Lascaux,
didn't the superstitious image their prey
into smoky home walls?

The aliens will argue, but never know
why, in the channel deep below,
extending forever into the darker tunnel north and south,
bipeds, now extinct, lay iron tracks.

twelve

More Mermaids

How do you make more mermaids
given the indivisible tail,
the invisible flower of generation?

Nor are the mermen any more scrutable.

Does each entwine, passing some juice
some elixir
between the pores, under the scales?
Are there organs in their hair, in their mouths,
in their hinder fins, pretty, iridescent, translucent,
filaments leading to the central belly
where tiny embryos recapitulate ontology?

Or do they pass love from the palms of their hands
a logical faculty: here, here is my seed
we shall have young.

Have you seen merbabies
fat wet cheeks
disneyesque foreshortening of the mer-grace
undulation of the majestic tail becoming mere
cute wriggles?
How do you diaper
that green scaly tail?

No: mermaids are immortal
a cross of ancient fishermen and sea-cats
sterile, beautiful, made ten thousand years ago
invincible to shark and barracuda.
Only the harpoon thrown in despair
only the gold shaft, loving, killing thrust
by the collector, the romantic boy
kills the mermaid.
There are fewer each year.

Things

Things
come into your life like medical students selling People magazine,
not what they pretend to be,
though you can never prove it.
This was Granny's antique relish dish, she says, neglecting
to mention your grandmother had forty-seven others very similar,
plus of course think of the enormous value
despite the poor glue job.
Grandma also collected umbrella stands and had a thing about pancakes.

Things stay,
like rust stains in the bathtub,
or like people you met in Put-In-Bay,
who drop in as you were gearing up to make love
or go to sleep or settle in front of the TV with cat in your lap.
And you end up knowing you can't give away
Mother's hand-crocheted tablecloth,
or the towels embroidered with ugly blue flowers,
Dad's seashell collection,
or the 1900's family photos with Uncle Bud or was it Aunt Alma,
wearing a drooping fedora or maybe a dead Maine Coon cat.
And there's the rolling pin, splintered,
which however rolled every pumpkin pie you ate
from birth to age 37.

Then things quietly leave,
like people at parties who have nothing to say,
like friends moving to Minnesota,
like kids who, thing by thing, desert the playroom.
A ring you took off because your hands swelled before Jacky came
suddenly isn't there when Jacky turns four.
Somebody must have broken the Limoge sugar
and threw away the creamer so you'd never notice,
and Mother insists she gave you, not Janey,
that tiger's eye brooch you remember only from dreams.

Things
matter
they are a way
more effective than people
of stopping time for a minute,
except they overstay
then just when you're getting to like them
they wait until you're busy on the telephone
and disappear into someplace
that gives you back only shabby towels
tarnished soupspoons and chipped china.
I think
it's called
the past.

The Hunter's Mothers

My new mother gave me milk in a bowl,
groomed me with her large smooth paws,
held me, not in her mouth like my first mother,
but in her big lap, where I fell asleep.

I watched her each day, carefully,
so she could teach me to groom,
and hunt, and mate, and do whatever
was catly for me to perform.

She cut meat that she had caught
somewhere, and put it on plates as big as me
for her other kittens, the large bald ones.
But she never let me have the knife

nor let me play with the meat. Was I unworthy?
I went to the door, thinking she would take me
out in the grass and teach me to hunt.
But she said no.

And when I did go out, she stayed inside
and taught me nothing of hunting.
Perhaps I was too small, my claws too blunt
to catch meat for her and her unfurry kittens.

With practice, I caught a small meaty thing
that wriggled until I batted it to stillness.
Rather than eat it at once, I took it to Mother.
She screamed and threw it away.

Was it not large enough?
Was it not good meat?
I could not get it out of the big can where she puts
uninteresting vegetables and bones.

Later I caught others, but never one she liked much
So I ate them myself, including
the ones that could fly, which I knew
Mother especially did not like.

I have lived a long time with Mother
Her two-legged kittens grew up big, and ran away.
She grooms me when I sit on her lap
but does not thank me for what I catch.

I know I am an unworthy hunter
but how could I learn, when she never taught me?
Maybe she knew I was not as clever as the big meat
that she catches to put on the high table.

So I sleep in a patch of sun
and dream of my first mother,
who went away, but first taught me
I have claws.

ACKNOWLEDGEMENTS

"Carpe Diem," *Lawn Party*, Fantome Press, 1988

"Corn Snake", *Asimov's*, February 2002

"Dark of the Moon," *Moscon Program Book*, September 1992

"Dash." *Tales of the Unanticipated*, #16, Spr-Sum-Fall '96

"Edward Curtis's Two Zuni Women," Ohio Poetry Day 1994 Winners, and *Dark Regions' The Year's Best Fantastic Fiction*, 3:2 1995

"Epithalamion," *Asimov's* Sept. 2002

"FAQ," *Lady Churchill's Rosebud Wristlet*, Jan. 2005

"Flowers Over Steel," *Lost and Found: An Anthology of Teacher's Writing*, Plymouth Writers Group, Fall 2003

"Foreigner," *1988 Odyssey Poetry Awards*, Provo, Utah: Brigham Young University, Spring 1988

"Hamsters," *Star*Line*, May/June 1992

"He Was Like," *Lawn Party*, Fantome Press, 1988

"Hydrangea," *Tributaries*, ed. Cyril Dostal and Jill Sell, 1997

"If You Loved Me," *Asimov's*, December, 1993

"La Brea Tar Pits: Early Summer, Dinnertime," *Star*Line* July/August 2005

"Lawnmowers" appeared in *Paper Blossom: An Anthology of Spring*, Avonelle, Columbus, 1978

"Mantis," *Tributaries*, ed. Cyril Dostal and Jill Sell, 1998

"Mollusks" appeared under the title "Crustaceans" in *Asimov's*, March 02

"More Mermaids," *Pandora*, Spring 1987

"More Ways to Tell If Your Cat Is a Space Alien," *Asimov's*, April 01

"My Dentist's Son," *Driftwood East* 4:4, Fall, 1976

"Off to the Big Time" was performed in January 1988 at Light, Space, & Time, a Mirror for the Arts at the Beck Center for the Cultural Arts in Cleveland, Ohio, to celebrate the 100th anniversary of the Michelson-Morley experiment. This book is its first print appearance.

"Past Lives, " *Worlds of Fantasy & Horror*, Summer 1994

"Sirens," *The Harrow*, Fall 2006

"St. E's Emergency," *Ev'ryman*, Deciduous Press, 2001

"Surrogate," *Star*Line*, May/June 2007

"The Deep," *Tributaries*, Ed. Cyril Dostal and Jill Sell, 1998

"The Hunter's Mothers," *Asimov's*, March 1998

"The Monster's Mother, " *Once upon a Midnight*, Unnameable Press '95

"Theater Moonie," *The New Kent Quarterly*, V.1, Fall 1979

"Tiptree" appeared as "Foundling" in *Tributaries*, Owl Walk Press, '97

APPEARING FOR THE FIRST TIME:

"An Indian Woman"

"Augmented"

"Botanist"

"Boxworld"

"Boxes of Poetry"

"Check Out Madonna"

"Consolations of Bast"

"December Morning"

"Early Space Traveler Fantasies"

"Foam Peanuts Float in Ditch"

"Gacy"

"God's Savagery in a Hospital Corridor"

"Gypsy and the Snake"

"Hibiscus Island, 2034 AD"

"Honey, You"

"How to Pick Berries"

"Metamorphosis of the English Teacher"

"Moon, Oh Luminous Companion"

"Old Poet Calls Me Up"

"Pasadena, July 4, 1997: Earth Invades Mars"

"Play/Ground"

"Rat"

"Road Kill"

"She Wasn't Afraid"

"She Who Was the Beautiful Helmut-Maker's Wife"

"Signs You're in Trouble"

"Snow after False Spring, Again"

"Some Joys Never Die"

"Suppose Heaven"

"Switchback Above Cat's Tail Creek"

"The Night They Blew the Thinker Up"

"The Telescope"

"The Tooth"

"The Tyrannosaur under 81st and 7th Avenue"

"Things"

"Thirteen Ways of Looking at a Blackbird Looking at a Black Cat"

"Tony"

"Two Girls Escaped"

"We Made Poetry"

vanZeno Press

www.vanzenopress.com

Through our Professional Reading Series, vanZeno Press publishes fine books of poetry that our editorial board believes meet high standards of excellence and deserve to be published; poetry written by poets who are serious about their work, and who actively read or perform their work at poetry readings and other events.
If you're interested in submitting a manuscript or in learning more about our publishing process, please take a look at the vanZeno website and if you're still interested, please send an inquiry letter with a sample of 5-10 poems to editor@vanzenopress.com.